AMAZING ANIMALS
OF THE WORLD ③

Volume 8

Salamander, Two-Lined — Spider, Barrel

GROLIER
an imprint of
SCHOLASTIC
Scholastic Library Publishing
www.scholastic.com/librarypublishing

First published 2006 by Grolier, an imprint of Scholastic Library Publishing

© 2006 Scholastic Library Publishing

For information address the publisher: Grolier, Scholastic Library Publishing
90 Old Sherman Turnpike
Danbury, CT 06816

10 digit: Set ISBN: 0-7172-6179–4; Volume ISBN: 0-7172-6187–5
13 digit: Set ISBN: 978-0-7172-6179–6; Volume ISBN: 978-0-7172-6187–1

Printed and bound in the U.S.A.

Library of Congress Cataloging-in-Publications Data:
Amazing animals of the world 3.
p.cm.
Includes indexes.
Contents: v. 1. Abalone, Black–Butterfly, Giant Swallowtail -- v. 2. Butterfly, Indian Leaf–Dormouse, Garden -- v. 3. Duck, Ferruginous–Glassfish, Indian -- v. 4. Glider, Sugar–Isopod, Freshwater -- v. 5. Jackal, Side-Striped–Margay -- v. 6. Markhor–Peccary, Collared -- v. 7. Pelican, Brown–Salamander, Spotted -- v. 8. Salamander, Two Lined–Spider, Barrel -- v. 9. Spider, Common House–Tuna, Albacore -- v. 10. Tunicate, Light-Bulb–Zebra, Grevy's.
ISBN 0–7172–6179–4 (set : alk. paper) -- ISBN 0–7172–6180–8 (v. 1 : alk. paper) -- ISBN 0–7172–6181–6 (v. 2 : alk. paper) -- ISBN 0-7172-6182–4 (v. 3 : alk. paper) -- ISBN 0-7172-6183–2 (v. 4 : alk. paper) -- ISBN 0-7172-6184–0 (v. 5 : alk. paper) -- ISBN 0-7172-6185–9 (v. 6 : alk. paper) -- ISBN 0-7172-6186–7 (v. 7 : alk. paper) -- ISBN 0-7172-6187–5 (v. 8 : alk. paper) -- ISBN 0-7172-6188–3 (v. 9 : alk. paper) -- ISBN 0-7172-6189–1 (v. 10 : alk.paper)
1. Animals--Juvenile literature. I. Grolier (Firm) II. Title: Amazing animals of the world three.
QL49.A455 2006
590—dc22
2006010870

About This Set

Amazing Animals of the World 3 brings you pictures of 400 exciting creatures, and important information about how and where they live.

Each page shows just one species, or individual type, of animal. They all fall into seven main categories, or groups, of animals (classes and phylums scientifically) identified on each page with an icon (picture)—amphibians, arthropods, birds, fish, mammals, other invertebrates, and reptiles. Short explanations of what these group names mean, and other terms used commonly in the set, appear on page 4 in the Glossary.

Scientists use all kinds of groupings to help them sort out the types of animals that exist today and once wandered the earth (extinct species). *Kingdoms*, *classes*, *phylums*, *genus*, and *species* are among the key words here that are also explained in the Glossary.

Where animals live is important to know as well. Each of the species in this set lives in a particular place in the world, which you can see outlined on the map on each page. And in those places, the animals tend to favor a particular habitat—an environment the animal finds suitable for life—with food, shelter, and safety from predators that might eat it. There they also find ways to coexist with other animals in the area that might eat somewhat different food, use different homes, and so on.

Each of the main habitats is named on the page and given an icon, or picture, to help you envision

it. The habitat names are further defined in the Glossary on page 4.

As well as being part of groups like species, animals fall into other categories that help us understand their lives or behavior. You will find these categories in the Glossary on page 4, where you will learn about carnivores, herbivores, and other types of animals.

And there is more information you might want about an animal—its size, diet, where it lives, and how it carries on its species—the way it creates its young. All these facts and more appear in the data boxes at the top of each page.

Finally, the set is arranged alphabetically by the most common name of the species. That puts most beetles, for example, together in a group so you can compare them easily.

But some animals' names are not so common, and they don't appear near others like them. For instance, the chamois is a kind of goat or antelope. To find animals that are similar—or to locate any species—look in the Index at the end of each book in the set (pages 45–48). It lists all animals by their various names (you will find the Giant South American River Turtle under Turtle, Giant South American River, and also under its other name— Arrau). And you will find all birds, fish, and so on gathered under their broader groupings.

Similarly, smaller like groups appear in the Set Index as well—butterflies include swallowtails and blues, for example.

Table of Contents
Volume 8

Glossary

Amphibians—species usually born from eggs in water or wet places, which change (metamorphose) into land animals. Frogs and salamanders are typical. They breathe through their skin mainly and have no scales.

Arctic and Antarctic—icy, cold, dry areas at the ends of the globe that lack trees but see small plants grown in thawed areas (tundra). Penguins and seals are common inhabitants.

Arthropods—animals with segmented bodies, hard outer skin, and jointed legs, such as spiders and crabs.

Birds—born from eggs, these creatures have wings and often can fly. Eagles, pigeons, and penguins are all birds, though penguins cannot fly through the air.

Carnivores—they are animals that eat other animals. Many species do eat each other sometimes, and a few eat dead animals. Lions kill their prey and eat it, while vultures clean up dead bodies of animals.

Cities, Towns, and Farms—places where people live and have built or used the land and share it with many species. Sometimes these animals live in human homes or just nearby.

Class—part or division of a phylum.

Deserts—dry, often warm areas where animals often are more active on cooler nights or near water sources. Owls, scorpions, and jack rabbits are common in American deserts.

Endangered—some animals in this set are marked as endangered because it is possible they will become extinct soon.

Extinct—these species have died out altogether for whatever reason.

Family—part of an order.

Fish—water animals (aquatic) that typically are born from eggs and breathe through gills. Trout and eels are fish, though whales and dolphins are not (they are mammals).

Forests and Mountains—places where evergreen (coniferous) and leaf-shedding (deciduous) trees are common, or that rise in elevation to make cool, separate habitats. Rain forests are different. (see Rain forests)

Fresh Water—lakes, rivers, and the like carry fresh water (unlike Oceans and Shores, where the water is salty). Fish and birds abound, as do insects, frogs, and mammals.

Genus—part of a family.

Grasslands—habitats with few trees and light rainfall. Grasslands often lie between forests and deserts, and they are home to birds, coyotes, antelope, and snakes, as well as many other kinds of animals.

Herbivores—these animals eat mainly plants. Typically they are hoofed animals (ungulates) that are common on grasslands, such as antelope or deer. Domestic (nonwild) ones are cows and horses.

Hibernators—species that live in harsh areas with very cold winters slow down their functions then and sort of sleep through the hard times.

Invertebrates—animals that lack backbones or internal skeletons. Many, such as insects and shrimp, have hard outer coverings. Clams and worms are also invertebrates.

Kingdom—the largest division of species. Commonly there are understood to be five kingdoms: animals, plants, fungi, protists, and monerans.

Mammals—these creatures usually bear live young and feed them on milk from the mother. A few lay eggs (monotremes like the platypus) or nurse young in a pouch (marsupials like opossums and kangaroos).

Migrators—some species spend different seasons in different places, moving to where more food, warmth, or safety can be found. Birds often do this, sometimes over long distances, but other types of animals also move seasonally, including fish and mammals.

Oceans and Shores—seawater is salty, often deep, and huge. In it live many fish, invertebrates, and even some mammals, such as whales. On the shore, birds and other creatures often gather.

Order—part of a class.

Phylum—part of a kingdom.

Rain forests—here huge trees grow among many other plants helped by the warm, wet environment. Thousands of species of animals also live in these rich habitats.

Reptiles—these species have scales, lungs to breathe, and lay eggs or give birth to live young. Dinosaurs are thought to have been reptiles, while today the class includes turtles, snakes, lizards, and crocodiles.

Scientific name—the genus and species name of a creature in Latin. For instance, Canis lupus is the wolf. Scientific names avoid the confusion possible with common names in any one language or across languages.

Species—a group of the same type of living thing. Part of an order.

Subspecies—a variant but quite similar part of a species.

Territorial—many animals mark out and defend a patch of ground as their home area. Birds and mammals may call quite small or quite large spots their territories.

Vertebrates—animals with backbones and skeletons under their skins

Two-Lined Salamander
Eurycea bislineata

Length: 2½ to 4¾ inches
Diet: insects, spiders, and
   other small invertebrates
Number of Eggs: 12 to 100

Home: eastern North America
Order: Salamanders and
   newts
Family: Lungless salamanders

  Fresh Water

Amphibians

© ANDREW ODUM / PETER ARNOLD, INC.

Two-lined salamanders are abundant in the woodland streams of eastern North America. This small, slender species is recognized by the broad yellow stripe that runs down its back. Two dark lines border this golden band, one on each side. Many two-lined salamanders are darkly speckled and have a brown, green, or orange hue to their skin. Their head is tiny, and their long, muscular tail is flattened from side to side.

While other salamanders crawl across the damp forest floor, the "two-liner" rarely leaves the stream in which it was born. It swims powerfully and rapidly, using its flattened tail as a paddle. During the day, the salamander hides on a streambed by tucking its small body under a submerged stone. At night, it hunts for small insects and crustaceans in the water and along its edges. When frightened, this shy creature rapidly disappears into deep water, resurfacing only when all is quiet and still.

After breeding, the female attaches her eggs to submerged rocks, logs, or plants. She usually remains nearby to guard her clutch until they hatch. Like tadpoles, her hatchlings, or "larvae," have no legs and breathe through gills. Most youngsters transform into adults in one to three years, when they are about 1¾ inches long. But some never "grow up," and live their entire lives in their immature, gilled form.

Purple Sandpiper
Calidris maritima

Length: 8 to 9 inches
Weight: 2 to 3 ounces
Diet: insects, spiders, crustaceans, mollusks, fish, seeds, and plants
Number of Eggs: usually 4

Home: Arctic and northern Atlantic coasts
Order: Waders and gull-like birds
Family: Sandpipers and their relatives

 Oceans and Shores

 Birds

© ROGER TIDMAN / CORBIS

The purple sandpiper does not seem to mind the bone-chilling Arctic winds. This stocky bird spends the winter farther north than any other Atlantic shorebird. It lives on rocky, wave-swept beaches, where it catches crabs and mollusks. Purple sandpipers also pick insects out of icy rock crevices near the shore.

These birds are named for their dark winter plumage. In summer, they wear a streaked, pale brown coat. Bird-watchers find purple sandpipers surprisingly tame. A person can easily approach close enough to see the bird's distinctive yellow legs and the small white ring around each eye.

In spring, purple sandpipers fly to the northernmost parts of their range, where they breed on the cold Arctic tundra. The males arrive first, spacing themselves evenly across the frozen landscape and establishing personal territories. Within each territory the male makes several scrapes in the ground among the lichens or herbs. The female chooses one of the scrapes for their nest. The mated pair lines the nest with a thick cushion of grass. After the female lays her eggs, the parents take turns warming them. Every purple sandpiper has a special "brood patch" of naked skin on its belly. The bare, warm skin helps keep the eggs warm in frigid weather. Just before the eggs hatch, the female deserts the nest. The father is left to tend the chicks on his own.

Smalltooth Sawfish
Pristis pectinata

Length: up to 25 feet
Weight: up to 1,000 pounds
Diet: bottom-dwelling animals and fish
Method of Reproduction: live-bearer

Home: Atlantic Ocean, Gulf of Mexico, Caribbean Sea, and Mediterranean Sea
Order: Rays
Family: Sawfish

 Oceans and Shores

 Fish

© YVES LANCEAU / NHPA

The smalltooth sawfish, also called the greater sawfish, is the largest of all sawfish. This creature appears to be half-ray, half-shark. With its flattened body and bulging eyes on top of its head, it looks somewhat like a ray. In other ways, it resembles a shark: it has two dorsal fins and a tail that sweeps from side to side. The smalltooth sawfish also has a rubbery backbone made of cartilage.

The most striking trait of the smalltooth sawfish is its long, flat snout, which is studded with 24 to 32 pairs of strong teeth. This "saw" measures about one-third the length of the animal's body and has two purposes. The first is to dig for food. The sawfish roots around the muddy floor of oceans or rivers, digging out worms and other bottom-dwelling animals. It uses great force when it stirs up the seafloor.

The sawfish also uses its saw-toothed snout as a weapon. It will enter a school of small fish and violently thrash its saw from side to side. It then has an easy time catching and eating the fish it has wounded or stunned. The sawfish can also turn its weapon on those who try to attack it. Fishermen know to be careful around this animal's slashing saw.

Smalltooth sawfish are found in the shallow waters of tropical and subtropical oceans. They spend most of their time on or near the ocean floor. These fish are especially abundant in bays and estuaries, where river water runs into the sea.

Cottony-Cushion Scale
Icerya purchasi

Length: ⅛ to ¼ inch (female); less than 1/16 inch (male)
Diet: plant juices
Method of Reproduction: egg layer

Home: native to Australia; introduced elsewhere
Order: Aphids, scale insects, and their relatives
Family: Giant scale insects

Cities, Towns, and Farms

Arthropods

In 1868 a tiny Australian insect called the cottony-cushion scale was accidentally introduced into California. The insect quickly found an abundant supply of food in the leaves and twigs of orange trees and other valuable fruit plants. The females used their mouthparts to pierce the leaf's tissues and feed on the plant's vital fluids. In just 20 years, the cottony-cushion scale nearly destroyed California's citrus industry.

In appearance the cottony-cushion scale bears little resemblance to other insects. In habits, however, it is very much an insect. After mating, the female secretes a large white cottony egg sac in which the eggs are laid. Each female lays from 600 to 1,000 bright red eggs. In summer the eggs hatch in a few days. During the winter, they can take two months to hatch!

The young scale quickly finds a leaf or twig on which to settle. As it feeds and grows, the creature molts several times, finally changing, or metamorphosing, into an adult.

Fortunately for California's citrus growers, the cottony-cushion scale has an enemy from its native Australia: *Rhodalia cardinalis*, a small ladybird beetle. In 1888 large numbers of these beetles were released in orchards. Within two years the ladybirds had eaten enough of the scales to eliminate the problem. The beetles are used to this day to keep the population of cottony-cushion scales under control.

Scheltopusik
Ophisaurus apodus

Length: 32 to 55 inches
Diet: snails, insects, small mammals, and other lizards
Number of Eggs: 6 to 12

Home: southeastern Europe and Asia Minor
Order: Lizards and snakes
Family: Anguids

 Forests and Mountains

 Reptiles

The scheltopusik is a reptile with the head of a lizard and the body of a snake. Its name is from the Russian *zhelto*, meaning "yellow," and *puzik*, meaning "belly." This is quite misleading because adult scheltopusiks are entirely brown, and juveniles are gray with dark bars.

The scheltopusik belongs to a group of lizards nicknamed glass snakes. Like the glass snakes of the United States, this species is nearly legless and has a hard, shiny armor of skin. On its belly are two little stumps that are the remnants of back legs. Over the centuries, the creature's front legs have disappeared entirely. So stiff is its armor that the lizard would not be able to

expand its body to breathe but for the deep, flexible grooves along the sides of the armor.

Scheltopusiks live on rocky hillsides, in dry meadows, and near the edges of sparse woodlands. Occasionally they sun themselves on rocks and stone walls. The lizard is most active in the early morning and evening and after rainstorms.

The female scheltopusik is a protective parent. After laying her clutch of eggs, she curls around it. She warms and guards her eggs for up to two months. After hatching, the young must fend for themselves. Many are eaten by predatory birds. Those that survive to adulthood may live 20 years.

Common Scorpionfly
Panorpa communis

Length: 0.6 to 0.8 inch
Diet: live and rotting plant and animal matter
Method of Reproduction: egg layer

Wingspan: 1⅕ inches
Home: Europe
Order: Scorpionflies
Family: Common scorpionflies

Forests and Mountains

Arthropods

Scorpionflies are neither scorpions nor flies. They are small insects that look like scorpions—the end of a male scorpionfly's abdomen is enlarged and turned upward in a scorpionlike manner. But unlike a scorpion, the scorpionfly does not have a stinger, and it cannot hurt humans.

Adult scorpionflies have two pairs of long, transparent wings. When a scorpionfly is resting, it holds its wings out horizontally—not vertically over its abdomen. On its head are very long antennae and huge eyes. There also is a long snout, or beak, at the end of which are mouthparts designed for biting and chewing.

Scorpionflies are usually found sitting on plants in moist, shady places along streams and in damp woods. They feed on a variety of foods, including plant juices, fruits, insects, and dead animal matter.

After mating, a female lays her eggs in the ground. The larvae that hatch from the eggs look like caterpillars. The larvae crawl over the ground, looking for small insects to eat. When they reach a certain size, the larvae burrow in the ground and enter a resting stage called the pupa. During this stage, the insects change, or metamorphose, into adults. A pupa moves up to the surface of the ground just before the adult is ready to spread its wings and fly.

Snubnose Sculpin
Orthonopias triacis

Length: up to 4 inches
Diet: probably crustaceans and small fish
Home: Pacific Ocean off the coasts of California and Baja California

Method of Reproduction: egg layer
Order: Mail-cheeked fishes
Family: Sculpins and bullheads

 Oceans and Shores

 Fish

© LAWRENCE NAYLOR / PHOTO RESEARCHERS

The snubnose sculpin is recognized by its short snout and closely packed scales on its head and back. The rest of its body is "naked," or scaleless. A snubnose may be green, reddish-brown, or orange. It has five colorful, saddle-shaped markings on its back, as well as many smaller spots.

Like other sculpins, this species has a large head and a relatively small body. It is generally considered to be too bony and too ugly to serve at the dinner table. In fact, in some places the word "sculpin" is used for a worthless creature or person.

Snubnose sculpin are rare and mysterious. Scientists do not know for certain what they eat. It is thought that sculpins are bottom feeders that hunt for small crustaceans and fish in the mud and sand. They seldom swim into deep water, preferring rocky shallows close to shore.

Scientists believe that snubnose sculpins spawn only between mid-March and mid-April. No one has ever actually seen this fish mate. However, studies done on the female show that she has an unusual way of fertilizing her eggs. She extends a special organ toward her mate to collect his "milt," or sperm. The female then draws the milt-covered organ back into her body. Later, when she is ready to lay her eggs, she fertilizes them herself with the stored sperm.

Beadlet Sea Anemone
Actinia equina

Diet: small fish, crustaceans, and organic matter
Method of Reproduction: egg layer

Width: about 2 inches
Home: eastern Atlantic Ocean
Order: True sea anemones
Family: Sea anemones

 Oceans and Shores

Other Invertebrates

© LAWSON WOOD / CORBIS

Anemones are sea creatures that resemble flowers. Their bodies are plump stalks, which are topped by several rings of flowery tentacles. Beadlet sea anemones are particularly colorful. Most are bright crimson, although some are green and brown or even striped and spotted.

The beadlet sea anemone is named for the tiny blue sacs at the base of its tentacles. These beads can be seen when the creature closes its "blossom." Sea anemones curl their tentacles, like a flower closing its petals, when they are exposed to air. This helps to keep their squishy bodies from drying out at low tide.

The sea anemone's tentacles are covered with stinging cells. Their prickly sting discourages predators from taking a bite. Even more important, the anemone stings to stun small prey. It then uses its tentacles to sweep the paralyzed victim into its mouth.

A beadlet sea anemone generally stays in one place. When it needs to move, the creature slowly inches and slides across the seabed. Sometimes pieces of the sea anemone break off as it moves. These bits can regenerate into small, new anemones, identical to their parent. Each sea anemone is both male and female, and forms both eggs and sperm inside its stomach. The anemone spits the eggs and sperm into the water when it wants to breed.

Dahlia Sea Anemone
Tealia felina

Diet: crustaceans and small
  fish
Method of Reproduction: egg
  layer
Diameter of Base: 2 inches

Diameter of Crown: 6 inches
Home: North Atlantic, Arctic,
  and North Pacific oceans
Order: Sea anemones
Family: Actiniid anemones

  Oceans and
Shores

Other
Invertebrates

© ANDREW J. MARTINEZ / PHOTO RESEARCHERS

The dahlia sea anemone is an animal that looks like a flower. But looks can be deceiving. The dahlia is definitely not a flower; rather, it is a voracious predator.

In the world of predators, there are those, such as tigers and sharks, that chase their prey. Then there are those that sit and wait for their prey to pass by, such as the dahlia anemone. Like all anemones, this species hunts with its tentacles. Some anemones eat only microscopic plants, animals, and bacteria. But the dahlia anemone can catch much larger prey.

The dahlia anemone can both smell and feel the movements of its prey as the prey floats through the water. If it senses the approach of a fish or crustacean, the dahlia anemone begins to wave the ring of tentacles around its mouth. Any small animal that stumbles into these undulating tentacles is stunned by tiny poison-tipped spears. The tentacles then sweep the paralyzed animal into the anemone's waiting mouth.

Anemones also use their tentacles and stingers to defend themselves against enemies. Touch a dahlia anemone, and you may receive a painful sting. Some crabs, however, have learned to exploit the anemone's sting. They often carry these little "flowers" on their shells to discourage any animal looking for a crab dinner.

Frilled Sea Anemone
Metridium senile

Length: 12 inches
Method of reproduction:
sexually by eggs and sperm;
asexually by dividing
lengthwise
Diet: tiny animals

Diameter of the crown: 8
inches
Home: Atlantic Ocean
Order: Typical sea anemones
Family: Metridiids

 Oceans and Shores

 Other Invertebrates

© HERB SEGARS / ANIMALS ANIMALS / EARTH SCENES

The sea anemone is a very strange-looking creature with a stout, muscular body. At the upper end is a mouth surrounded by hollow tentacles that look like the petals of a chrysanthemum or other flower. A large frilled sea anemone may have as many as 1,000 delicate tentacles. It uses the tentacles to catch tiny organisms and bring them to its mouth. The tentacles are armed with special stinging cells, which discharge long white threads when anything brushes against them. The threads help to capture and subdue prey. If the sea anemone is disturbed or exposed to air during low tide, it pulls its tentacles inward, over its mouth, and contracts the upper part of its body—much like pulling your lips into your mouth.

Frilled sea anemones are common in shallow waters along the coasts of the Atlantic Ocean, from tide pools and the low-tide line to a depth of about 500 feet. They often attach themselves to rocks, wharf pilings, and other solid objects. A frilled sea anemone can slowly glide on its slimy base, or disk.

Sea anemones reproduce sexually by forming eggs and sperm. They also reproduce asexually by dividing in half lengthwise. Sometimes, as a sea anemone creeps along, it leaves behind bits of its disk. These small pieces can regenerate into new sea anemones.

Sea Hare
Aplysia punctata

Length: about 5 inches
Diet: seaweed
Method of Reproduction: egg layer
Number of Eggs: up to 500

Home: the shores of the Atlantic Ocean and nearby seas
Order: Tectibranch
Family: Sea hares

Oceans and Shores

Other Invertebrates

The sea hare lives in muddy or sandy areas near the shore. There it swims around on its back, using short muscular contractions to move itself forward. The sea hare has four tentacles that scientists think are actually organs of taste. The creature sees by means of eyes located at the base of the two rear tentacles. The front two tentacles resemble rabbit ears. It is this feature of the sea hare that gave the creature its name. The sea hare bears a much closer resemblance to a slug than to a rabbit. It is a yellowish or greenish animal. It has lobes on its sides that are used as fins, and it breathes by means of gills. The sea hare feeds primarily on seaweed, which it chews using its strong jaws and muscular lips. In the spring, vast numbers of sea hares move close to the beach to spawn (lay eggs). The eggs are laid in pink, spaghettilike strings that are coiled around rocks and weeds.

The sea hare's shell, not visible from the outside, is thin, transparent, and flexible, and probably offers the creature little, if any, protection. The sea hare must therefore rely on chemical protection. When handled or otherwise disturbed, the sea hare discharges a purple fluid from special glands that tastes bad to predators. This substance, because it irritates the skin of humans, led ancient peoples to believe that the sea hare is poisonous. Actually, the sea hare is harmless, and in some places, sea hare is considered a tasty dish.

Phosphorescent Sea Pen
Pennatula phosphorea

Length: 4 to 12 inches
Diet: plankton and organic matter
Methods of Reproduction: egg laying and cloning

Home: coasts of the Atlantic Ocean and Mediterranean Sea
Order: Sea pens
Family: Winglike sea pens

 Oceans and Shores

Other Invertebrates

© B. JONES & M. SHIMLOCK / NHPA

Just one look at this creature reveals how it was named! The feathery part of the sea pen's body, which looks like the end of an old-fashioned quill pen, is actually a colony of many tiny animals called polyps. Some of the polyps gather food, while others breathe for the entire colony. The individual polyps are arranged in "featherlets," which are attached to the colony's stiff center pole, or "quill."

Sea pens stand upright, with the end of their long quill buried in the sand. A sea pen lying flat on the ground can bend the tip of its quill downward, making a small hollow in the sand. It then pushes the quill tip deeper and deeper. Once it is well anchored, the sea pen jerks its entire "body"

upright. Sometimes it must uproot itself and crawl about in search of food.

The phosphorescent sea pen is one of the most beautiful of its kind. It is thinner and more delicate than others in its family. Normally this sea pen's "feather" is a brilliant yellow with a reddish center stalk. But when disturbed, the entire colony produces a strong greenish-blue glow. This creature has no true light-producing organs. Instead it creates a glow by releasing tiny, radiant grains from its sticky skin. The grains produce light only when they come in contact with water. When the sea pen is touched, its glow slowly spreads from the point of contact across its entire body.

Crabeater Seal
Lobodon carcinophagus

Length: up to 9 feet
Weight: about 500 pounds
Diet: euphausids (small crustaceans)
Number of Young: 1

Home: waters and ice around Antarctica
Order: Pinnipeds
Family: Earless seals

  Arctic and Anarctic

Mammals

© GALEN ROWELL / CORBIS

Despite its name the crabeater seal never eats crabs. Instead, its diet consists of small crustaceans called euphausids (commonly known as krill). The seal usually feeds at night while swimming through the icy waters around Antarctica. When the crabeater seal finds a school of krill, it opens its mouth to take in a gulp of water. As the seal expels the water through the sides of its mouth, it uses its teeth as a strainer to capture the krill that are now ready to be swallowed.

The crabeater is the most common of all seals, but rarely seen by Americans because of its remote habitat. Although its main enemies are the killer whale and the leopard seal, bad weather and starvation kill many young crabeater seals before predators even get a chance.

In the Antarctic spring (September through November), the female gives birth to her pups right on the ice—a chilly entrance into the world! At birth a pup is about 4½ feet long and weighs about 50 pounds. Several weeks after the pup is born, the adult seals mate in order to begin the cycle anew.

The crabeater seal molts every fall. During this process the old coat is replaced with a new grayish-brown coat. But as the months pass, the fur gets lighter and lighter. By the following summer, the coat is a creamy white, matching the color of the seal's icy home.

Southern Elephant Seal
Mirounga leonina

Length: 13 to 16 feet (male); 6½ to 10 feet (female)
Weight: up to 8,800 pounds (male); up to 2,900 pounds (female)
Diet: squid and fish

Number of Young: 1
Home: islands and archipelagoes in Antarctic waters and Tierra del Fuego
Order: Carnivores
Family: Earless seals

  Arctic and Anarctic

Mammals

© DAVID HOSKING / PHOTO RESEARCHERS

The longest, and by far the heaviest, seal in the world is the 4-ton male southern elephant seal. The name "elephant" refers not only to the male seal's massive size, but also to his trunklike nose. During breeding season the mature male, called a bull, inflates his trunk with air and blood pressure. He uses his big nose to intimidate other males and to attract females. Weighing only 1 ton, female elephant seals look like children next to the enormous males.

In September the southern elephant seal leaves the frigid Antarctic waters to give birth on land. During this time, 30 to 40 females, called cows, form a harem around one male leader. Their pups grow rapidly, gaining as much as 20 pounds a day during the weeks that their mothers nurse them. About the time her pups are weaned, the mother seal mates with the bull who heads her harem. Then the southern elephant seals—bulls, cows, and pups—all crash into the water to hunt for food. They swim far from shore and dive deep beneath the surface to find squid and fish.

In the 19th century, hunters killed so many southern elephant seals that it looked as if the species would become extinct. But in 1964 the world's countries agreed to protect this animal. Since then the seal population has rebounded, and their survival seems assured.

Weddell Seal
Leptonychotes weddelli

Length: up to 10 feet
Weight: up to 1,100 pounds
Diet: mainly fish
Number of Young: 1

Home: coasts of Antarctica
Order: Carnivores
Family: Earless seals

Arctic and Anarctic

Mammals

© PETER JOHNSON / CORBIS

Weddell seals are champion divers. They commonly dive to depths of 1,000 to 1,300 feet and stay underwater for 20 minutes at a time. One Weddell seal that was fitted with a depth gauge dove to a depth of 1,900 feet and stayed underwater for 70 minutes! Like people, seals breathe air. But a seal's body has special features to keep water from entering the lungs and to allow the seal to remain underwater for long periods of time. It can close its nostrils and slow its heartbeat, thus using less oxygen.

Weddell seals spend almost all their time in water. In winter, they often remain below the ice, getting air either through cracks in the ice or from air pockets. Their voices can be heard as they call to one another beneath the ice. When swimming, Weddell seals propel themselves by moving their back flippers up and down. These creatures move clumsily on land because their back flippers cannot be turned forward and tucked under their body.

A few days before she gives birth, the female seal climbs onto solid ice near the Antarctic coast. Her newborn weighs 55 pounds or more. The mother nurses the pup for five or six weeks. Her milk is extremely rich, and the baby gains weight rapidly. Gradually, the mother introduces her baby to water by taking the pup into shallow pools on the ice. Later the young animal begins to enter the sea and catches its own food.

Allis Shad
Alosa alosa

Length: up to 27 inches
Diet: plant and animal plankton
Method of Reproduction: egg layer

Home: coastal waters of Europe
Order: Herrings and their relatives
Family: Herrings

 Oceans and Shores

 Fish

© BERTHOULE / JACANA / PHOTO RESEARCHERS

The allis shad does not have teeth. To obtain food, this fish sucks in water through its mouth and into its throat. The throat of the allis shad is lined with 60 to 80 thin, long gill rakers. The rakers strain out tiny organisms from the water. These organisms can then be easily swallowed and digested by the fish. The water also passes over the fish's gills, which extract oxygen. Finally, the water, minus its food and oxygen content, is passed out of an opening in the side of the shad's head.

During the winter, allis shad live in the open sea. In early spring, they band together in large groups called shoals and migrate up European rivers to spawn. At the chosen breeding ground, the female drops her eggs into the water as her mate releases his sperm, which fertilizes the eggs. The eggs sink to the bottom of the riverbed. In about a week, the eggs hatch, and the adults return to the sea. The young shad, however, may spend up to two years in the river where they were born before swimming downstream to the sea.

Allis shad are large, tasty fish with an oily flesh. In the past, people caught them in great numbers. They were once much more common in European rivers than they are today. Overfishing and the effects of water pollution on their environment have greatly reduced their populations.

Cookiecutter Shark
Isistius brasiliensis

Length: 6 to 20 inches
Diet: other sharks, whales, squid, porpoises, and tuna
Method of Reproduction: unknown

Home: warm regions of the Atlantic, Pacific, and Indian oceans
Order: Dogfish sharks
Family: Dogfish sharks

 Oceans and Shores

 Fish

© NORBERT WU / PETER ARNOLD, INC.

The cookiecutter shark is named after its gruesome eating habits. This small, aggressive shark uses its suckerlike lips to attach itself to the sides of tuna, whales, and other large animals. Then it uses its teeth to cut out circular "cookies" of flesh. Many victims manage to free themselves and escape, but for the rest of their lives they bear circular scars where they were attacked by the cookiecutter.

Like other sharks, the cookiecutter's entire skeleton is made of cartilage. The shark does not have a single bone in its body. Even its teeth are cartilage, covered with a very hard material. The teeth of the upper and lower jaws are different. The upper teeth are narrow spikes. The lower teeth are larger and extremely sharp; they overlap to form a sawlike structure. This structure is so sharp that it is difficult for people to catch cookiecutters. The sharks can quickly chew their way through a net and escape. A cookiecutter's teeth are not permanent. They constantly fall out and are replaced by new teeth. Sometimes an entire row of teeth is lost at once. The cookiecutter shark may swallow its own teeth if they fall out while it is eating.

Some people call this animal the luminous shark because it gives off a bright-green light from its belly. The purpose of the light is not known. Perhaps the light attracts prey, which the cookiecutter then attacks.

Barbary Sheep
Ammotragus lervia

Length: 4½ to 5½ feet
Weight: 60 to 320 pounds
Diet: bushes, grasses, and herbs
Home: North Africa and Morocco

Number of Young: 1 to 2
Order: Even-toed hoofed ungulates
Family: Bovides
Subfamily: Sheep and goats
Suborder: Ruminants

 Forests and Mountains

 Mammals

© HANS REINHARD / BRUCE COLEMAN INC.

Barbary sheep are born to jump. A surefooted kid can climb over the steep rocks of its mountain home almost immediately after its birth. As an adult, the sheep are able to leap more than 6 feet high from a standing start. In the rocky desert mountains of the Sahara, Barbary sheep climb to altitudes of 12,200 feet. Like most animals in this sunny, dry region, Barbary sheep spend most of the day resting in the shade. Their brown, shaggy coats blend perfectly with bare rock. In the evening, small groups of Barbary sheep descend to the valley floor where they feed on grass and herbs until the next morning.

Barbary bucks often duel over territory and females. They butt heads, as other wild sheep and goats do. They also horn wrestle. Standing head to head, two bucks try to interlock horns by turning their heads slowly to the side. In this way, one buck pulls his opponent backward by one horn and then tries to wrestle him to the ground.

Barbary sheep have probably been hunted ever since humans first picked up a spear. Today, Barbary sheep are disappearing from their native Africa. However, they breed so well in zoos that the extra animals are sometime released into the wild. As a result, there are now large populations of semi-wild Barbary sheep in parts of Texas, New Mexico, and southern California.

Northern Shoveler
Anas clypeata

Length: 17 to 22 inches
Diet: aquatic vegetation and insects
Number of Eggs: 10

Home: North America, Europe, and Asia
Order: Ducklike birds
Family: Surface-feeding ducks

 Fresh Water

 Birds

© DARRELL GULIN / CORBIS

The northern shoveler has a unique bill shaped like a large spoon. The bill serves these ducks well in foraging for food. The shoveler feeds on small aquatic animals and plants, straining water through comblike teeth along the sides of its bill. These ducks are "dabblers"; that is, they skim their food from the surface of the water, rarely diving except to escape a predator.

Northern shovelers breed throughout most of Europe, in parts of Asia, and in North America from western Alaska south to California and east to the Great Lakes. They prefer shallow fresh water, especially in muddy or marshy areas. They usually are seen in small flocks or pairs A colorful bird,

both sexes of northern shoveler show blue upper wings and white underwings while in flight. Female northern shovelers are speckled brown. At breeding time the male has a glossy green head with a brownish-black crown. The female makes a characteristic quacking call, with the first note the loudest. The male emits a series of low notes while courting.

It may take the female shoveler several weeks to find the perfect site for a nest. The nest tends to be in grassy areas away from water. The female lays eggs daily, reaching a total of about 10. The eggs hatch in 21 to 28 days. The ducklings follow their mother and find their own food until they venture out on their own about two months later.

Pistol Shrimp
Apheus macrocheles

Length: 1½ inches
Diet: tiny bits of animal and vegetable matter
Method of Reproduction: egg layer

Home: Atlantic Ocean, Gulf of Mexico, Caribbean Sea, and the Mediterranean Sea
Order: Decapods
Family: Shrimp

 Oceans and Shores

 Other Invertebrates

© MARK SMITH / PHOTO RESEARCHERS

The pistol shrimp gets its name from the unusual way it captures prey: it shoots a sharp stream of water with its snapping pincer (claw). This spraying action is accompanied by a popping noise that sounds like gunfire. The combination of water blast and loud noise, enough to stun the tiny animals on which it preys, also helps to scare away predators looking for a shrimp dinner. The pistol shrimp also feeds on bits of plant matter and occasionally scavenges for food.

Pistol shrimp belong to the order Decapoda, which means "10 legs." Only the first pair of legs on the pistol shrimp are equipped with pincers. The pincers are not the same size. Instead, one pincer, either left or right, is much larger. Pistol shrimp also use their legs to dig holes in which they live in pairs. The holes they make are often shared with fish. Some pistol shrimp have even been known to burrow into live sponges!

Pistol shrimp live in warm waters and in coral reefs—all places where food and hiding places are plentiful. Like all shrimp, the pistol shrimp has a three-part body consisting of a head, thorax (trunk), and abdomen (tail). Red-and-white-banded antennae, small eyes, and a small beak are on the head. The legs grow from the thorax. The abdomen bears tiny flattened limbs called swimmerets (swimming legs) and terminates in a finlike tail fan at the very end.

Lesser Siren
Siren intermedia

Length: up to 16 inches
Diet: worms and other small animals
Method of Reproduction: egg layer

Home: southeastern United States
Order: Salamanders and newts
Family: Sirens

  Fresh Water

Amphibians

© JOSEPH T. COLLINS / PHOTO RESEARCHERS

The lesser siren is an unusual kind of salamander. It has a long, eel-like body with large, feathery gills bunched together on the sides of the neck. Unlike most salamanders, the siren never loses its gills, which are used to remove oxygen from water, even though it also has lungs and breathes air. The front legs are small and weak; there are no back legs. A pointed tail makes up about one-third of its length.

Lesser sirens spend their entire lives in water. During the day, they hide among dense patches of weeds or remain buried in debris at the bottom of ponds, ditches, and swamps. They hunt at night, feeding on such aquatic animals as worms, crayfish, and snails. Sirens have no jawbones and no

teeth. A hard lining on the lips is used to hold and crush prey.

If the body of water in which lesser sirens live evaporates during dry weather, they burrow deep into the mud. Skin glands secrete a substance that forms a dry covering, or cocoon, around the entire body except the mouth. This protects the siren from dehydration. The siren may enter a period of inactivity called estivation, during which its heart rate and other body processes slow down. This enables the animal to conserve water as well as energy. A siren can survive in this condition for several months, until rains refill its habitat with water.

African Striped Skink
Mabuya striata

Length: 7 to 10 inches
Diet: insects, worms, and
    other invertebrates
Number of Young: 3 to 9

Home: eastern and southern
    Africa
Order: Lizards and snakes
Family: Skinks

 Grasslands

 Reptiles

© K. H. SWITAK / PHOTO RESEARCHERS

The striped skink is a familiar sight in and around African villages. Unafraid of humans, it prowls garden paths, perches on walls, and scurries in and out of open windows. A striped skink is constantly searching for food, usually insects and other invertebrates. Generally villagers and townspeople tolerate this reptile visitor because it rids their households of many pests. Nonetheless, a striped skink will bite the hand that tries to catch it.

The African striped skink is named for the two pale bands that run along either side of its dark body. In young individuals the stripes are distinctive and start above each eye and extend to the tail. But the stripes fade as the skink ages. Many adult striped skinks have no stripes at all. Most are gray, black, or brown, but some are a beautiful bronze red. All have smooth, sleek scales with a handsome, glossy sheen.

In the wild, the skinks live in a variety of habitats—from the damp edges of mangrove swamps to parched savannas. They are active throughout the day and spend much of the time in trees and on cliffs.

In the warmer regions of Central Africa, striped skinks breed year-round. In the south, females give birth only in the summer. The newborn measure about two inches and are independent almost immediately after birth.

Ground Skink
Scincella lateralis

Length: up to 4¾ inches
Diet: insects
Home : southeastern United States

Number of Young: 1 to 5
Order: Lizards
Family: Skinks

 Forests and Mountains

 Reptiles

© BUDDY MAYS / CORBIS

The ground skink is a small lizard. It lives in the southeastern part of the United States, where it makes its home near streams or in wooded areas. Here, with its smooth brownish scales, it can easily hide under rocks, leaves, or fallen trees. It hibernates during the winter, and it is not easy to spot during the other seasons of the year.

Despite its short, tiny legs, the ground skink is fast. When it runs to hide or to catch insects, it moves with a snakelike motion, almost slithering along the ground. It grabs the insects with its sharp, pointed teeth. If a predator grabs the ground skink's tail, the tail breaks off. While the predator is watching the still-wriggling tail, the skink darts away. It will grow a new tail, but the new appendage will not be as long as the old one. When most animals close their eyelids, they cannot see. But the ground skink can see even if its lower eyelids are raised over its eyes. This is because the ground skink, like other lizards, has eyelids with transparent "windows." This enables the skink to dig under leaves without getting dirt in its eyes.

The female ground skink lays between one and five eggs under a rock or a log during the summer. The eggs hatch about two months later.

Ocellated Skink
Chalcides ocellatus

Length: 6 to 12 inches
Home: Sardinia, Sicily, Malta, Greece, Crete, northern Africa, and southwestern Asia

Diet: mainly insects and spiders
Number of Young: usually 3
Order: Lizards and snakes
Family: Skinks

 Grasslands

 Reptiles

© ALLEN BLAKE SHELDON / ANIMALS ANIMALS / EARTH SCENES

The ocellated skink is named for the many black-edged eyespots, or "ocelli," on its sides. It is a plump and shiny lizard, of medium size, with a long, tapering tail. The creature has a very small head with a thick neck that blends evenly with the rest of its stout body. Like most skinks, this species is covered with smooth, overlapping scales that give it a sturdy, yet quite glossy appearance.

Ocellated skinks prefer dry, sandy habitats. In Greece and on the islands in the Mediterranean Sea, these lizards are fairly abundant in vineyards and on exposed farm fields. They are also found in coastal scrublands. Ocellated skinks warm up quickly in the morning sun and are most active in the hours after sunrise and just before sunset.

Despite its tiny legs, this skink can chase down its prey with lightning speed. Its small legs and feet are strong enough to dig underground tunnels, which provide shelter from the midday sun, as well as from the night cold.

Ocellated skinks are harmless to humans. Farmers appreciate the lizard's appetite for insect pests, and many children keep the reptile as a terrarium pet. In the mild climate of the Mediterranean, ocellated skinks breed several times a year. The female gives birth to live young, which she guards for only a short while.

Skylark
Alauda arvensis

Length: 6 to 8 inches
Weight: 1½ ounces
Diet: seeds, shoots, insects, and earthworms
Number of Eggs: 4 or 5

Home: native to Europe and Asia; introduced elsewhere
Order: Perching birds
Family: Larks

 Grasslands

 Birds

© PAUL HOBSON / FOTO NATURA / MINDEN PICTURES

Skylarks are renowned in music and literature for their beautiful singing. Even in flight the skylark emits lovely series of trills and breathtaking sequences of notes. A single song can last up to 10 minutes!

Nearly as spectacular as its music is the enchanting display the male skylark puts on during mating season. First, he runs around the female, raising his tail and fluffing up the small crest of feathers on his head. Then he takes to the air and begins to sing. He hovers for a while and then rises higher and higher in the sky, only to come spiraling downward, singing all the time. The male's behavior does more than just impress the by now awestruck female: it also acts to establish the skylark's territory.

Skylarks spend most of their time on the ground, living in open places such as farmland, meadows, and sandy coasts. Their large feet and long claws are well adapted for running, walking, and jumping. When a skylark senses danger, it tries to hide by crouching down and blending in with the surroundings.

Skylarks are excellent parents. The female incubates the eggs for 11 days in a nest built out of dry grasses. The young birds begin to leave the nest when they are about 10 days old, although their parents feed them until the babies are able to care for themselves.

Atlantic Slipper Shell
Crepidula fornicata

Length: 1 to 2½ inches
Width: up to 1 inch
Diet: tiny food particles filtered from the water
Method of Reproduction: egg layer

Home: eastern North America; introduced elsewhere
Order: Mesogastropods
Family: Slipper shells and their relatives

Oceans and Shores

Other Invertebrates

© ANDREW J. MARTINEZ / PHOTO RESEARCHERS

If you walk along a beach on the East Coast of North America, you are likely to see Atlantic slipper shells. The empty shells are often washed up onto beaches. They are shaped like a cap or an arched slipper. On the inside of the shell, there is a platform, or deck, that extends over the back half. This gives the animal two other common names: quarterdeck and boat shell. The platform looks like the quarterdeck of a sailing ship of long ago. Children often collect the shells and use them as tiny boats, sailing them in seaside pools. The shells also make handy little shovels for digging in the sand.

Living Atlantic slipper shells can be a nuisance. They can be so common in oyster beds that they smother the oysters. But empty slipper shells are useful. Oyster farmers scatter tons of the empty shells over the ocean floor. The shells form a "stool" on which young oysters can settle and grow.

Atlantic slipper shells live in shallow water. They attach themselves to hard objects, including rocks and other slipper shells. They often live in clusters. The largest—and therefore the oldest— individuals are at the bottom of the cluster. At the top are the smallest, youngest individuals. The slipper shell has a curious life cycle. When it is young, it is a male. As it gets older, it turns into a female.

Great Slug
Limax maximus

Length: 5 to 6 inches
Diet: fungi and decaying matter
Method of Reproduction: egg layer

Home: Europe and North America
Order: Land snails and slugs
Family: Limacid slugs

 Cities, Towns, and Farms

 Other Invertebrates

© DONALD SPECKER / ANIMALS ANIMALS / EARTH SCENES

Pick up a rock in a garden or look under a log at the edge of woodlands; that's where you may find a great slug. These small invertebrates feed at night and on cool, cloudy days. They hide on warm, sunny days. Many slugs eat plants and are garden pests, but the great slug is often called "the gardener's friend." It is a big eater, but it does not eat healthy green plants. Instead, it feeds mainly on fungi and dead, decaying organisms.

The great slug is usually pale brown or gray with black spots. It creeps along on a slimy trail of mucus, which is produced by a special mucus gland. The animal has two pairs of tentacles. Eyes are located at the tip of the back pair. The tentacles also contain the smell organs. As the slug travels, it moves its tentacles in every direction. In cold weather the slug hibernates. It crawls into a protected place and curls up into a ball. It secretes enough mucus to cover itself in a slimy envelope.

During courtship, two great slugs do a slow circle "dance." Then they crawl up a shrub or tree and onto a branch, where they attach a thread of mucus. They move down this thread and mate in midair. Each slug has both female and male organs. When they mate, they exchange sperm. Later each slug fertilizes its eggs with the sperm it received and then lays the eggs.

Sea Slug
Aeolidia papillosa

Length: up to 4 inches
Diet: anemones and sea pens
Method of Reproduction: egg layer

Home: all northern oceans
Order: Nudibranchs
Family: Aeolidiids

 Oceans and Shores

Other Invertebrates

Sea slugs are abundant in tidal pools and on beaches below the high-tide line. This creature is also called the "shag rug aeolis," because of the long, furlike tentacles that cover its body. (An aeolis is a type of slug.) The sea slug's "hairs" are actually bits of skin that work like gills. The sea slug breathes through them. Because the tentacles are connected to the slug's gut, they take on the color of whatever the slug has eaten. As a result a sea slug can easily hide among the animals that it eats.

Sea anemones are by far the sea slug's favorite meal. Anemones are flowerlike animals with stinging tentacles that look like flower petals. Using its bladelike jaws, the sea slug takes large, vicious bites from the base of the anemone. The slug tries to avoid the stinging petals at the top of the anemone's stalk. However, the sea slug has a tough throat that can withstand a little anemone poison. The slug's body actually saves some of the anemone's poison, which travels into the tips of its own tentacles. In these cases the sea slug has the sting, as well as the color, of its food.

All sea slugs have both eggs and sperm inside their body. They take turns fertilizing each other's eggs. When they hatch, the offspring are tiny swimming creatures that float out with the tide. Eventually they grow large enough to sink to the sea bottom and develop into adult slugs.

Common Snail
Helix aspersa

Length: 1¼ inches
Weight: up to 2 ounces
Home: Central and southwestern Europe, East and West coasts of the United States, and Texas

Diet: twigs, leaves, and grass
Number of Eggs: 40
Order: Terrestrial snails
Family: Spiral-shelled terrestrial snails

 Cities, Towns, and Farms

 Other Invertebrates

© GEORGE D. LEPP / CORBIS

The common snail is often called the "common pest" of Europe. And the Europeans have now shared this little curse with many countries. The common snail has hitched many international rides while hidden in the leaves of potted plants. It spends its days munching on plant leaves and otherwise making a mess of flower gardens and vegetable patches.

Like other land snails, the common snail slides from leaf to leaf on a film of slimy liquid. This slime oozes from the snail's flat, fleshy "foot," which extends from its shell. The goo is sticky and temporarily glues the foot in place. This enables the snail to pull its body forward. It then lifts its foot slightly and slides it forward again.

The slow pace of this slip-and-slide gives us the expression "to move at a snail's pace."

The common snail, like most land snails, is not separated into different sexes. Each snail has both male and female sex organs. That means they can both lay eggs and fertilize another snail's eggs. When two common snails mate, they press the soles of their feet together. They then pierce each other's body with tiny darts, dubbed "love arrows." After fertilization takes place through this connection, the snails deposit their eggs in a hole in the soil. The common snail's eggs have a rich yolk that provides food for the developing young. The babies emerge as tiny but fully developed copies of their parents.

Pond Snail
Lymnaea stagnalis

Length: 2 inches
Diet: animal, plants, and algae
Home: North America and Europe

Number of Eggs: 2 to 100
Order: Pond snails
Family: Lymnaeidae

Fresh Water

Other Invertebrates

© I. MOAR / OSF / ANIMALS ANIMALS / EARTH SCENES

Great pond snails live throughout Europe and North America in freshwater ponds, lakes, rivers, and ditches. They prefer water less than two feet deep and come to the surface at regular intervals to breathe. When they are unable to reach the surface because of ice or some other object, they can survive by breathing through their skin.

The size of the snail's shell depends upon how strong the water current is. When the snails inhabit weeds or rushes, their shells become indented around the opening. Generally, the high, coiled shells are dark brown. The snail's eyes are at the base of two flat tentacles. The pond snail has a unique mantle tissue that it can spread outside its shell and all but cover itself, making the creature appear like a wad of glue. This way the snail can hide from predators.

Pond snails creep along by waves of muscular contractions. Sometimes they crawl upside down at the surface of the water. They break their food into tiny fragments with a filelike tongue covered with thousands of teeth.

Each individual snail has male and female organs; and though they do mate, a single snail is capable of forming a colony. They lay their eggs in jellylike masses. Each mass may contain from 2 to 100 eggs, which hatch within two or three weeks.

Checkered Keelback Snake
Xenochropis piscator

Diet: fish, frogs, and small snakes
Method of Reproduction: egg layer

Length: up to 4 feet
Home: southern Asia
Order: Lizards and snakes
Family: Colubrid snakes

  Fresh Water

Reptiles

© C.B. FRITH / BRUCE COLEMAN INC.

The keelback snake is "checkered" with rows of square black spots. Its back is covered with scales that overlap like roof shingles. The rear edge of each scale is "keeled," or angled slightly upward. The checkered keelback snake's most distinctive marking is a pair of black stripes that angle downward from each eye. The creature's large eyes and round pupils are unusual; most snakes have vertical pupils.

The checkered keelback snake often lives in Asian rice paddies and irrigation ditches. It also inhabits swamps and the lush banks of jungle rivers. This long, slender snake is a fast and skillful swimmer. Although it is not venomous, the keelback is an efficient predator. It catches small fish underwater and frogs and small snakes along the shore.

Sometimes Asian farm workers accidentally step on the keelback. Fortunately, it is not aggressive and seeks only to escape. But if provoked, it will bite deeply and repeatedly. It will also strike at any animal that corners it.

After mating near water, the female keelback hides her eggs under wet, fallen leaves and bent reeds. She always lays her eggs near a pool of water or on the outskirts of a swamp. In this way, her hatchlings can effortlessly slip into the water soon after they are born.

False Coral Snake
Anilius scytale

Diet: amphibians, lizards, and small snakes
Method of Reproduction: live bearer

Length: about 30 inches
Home: South America
Order: Lizards and snakes
Family: Annelids

 Rain forests

Reptiles

© JUAN MANUEL RENJIFO / ANIMALS ANIMALS / EARTH SCENES

Like true coral snakes, this slender, colorful serpent is marked with black bands on a reddish background. Some varieties of false coral snake look speckled or shimmery because their red scales are edged in black. But unlike true coral snakes, which are deadly poisonous, false coral snakes are quite harmless.

The false coral snake is also known as the "two-headed" snake. In shape, its rounded tail resembles its head. In order to defend itself, the snake hides its true head and waves its decoy tail. When the attacker strikes at the tail, the false coral snake has a chance to escape with only a minor wound.

False coral snakes love the rain and are most active when the ground is slippery and wet. They are nighttime hunters that catch burrowing amphibians and reptiles. Among their favorite meals are toads and small snakes. During the day, the false coral snake hides in the sand. It digs a shallow burrow in loose, dry soil. After mating, the female false coral snake keeps her eggs inside her body, where they hatch. She gives birth to live snakes, which she guards for a brief time.

The false coral snake is the only member of its family (Annelidae) to be found in the Americas. Its cousins, the pipe snakes, are common in Asia. All annelids are harmless tropical snakes that burrow into the ground.

Indonesian Rat Snake
Ptyas korros

Length: up to 6 feet
Diet: rodents, birds, frogs, lizards, and other vertebrates
Number of Young: 6 to 9

Home: Southeast Asia
Order: Lizards and snakes
Family: Common snakes
Suborder: Snakes

 Grasslands

 Reptiles

© DAVID M. DENNIS / ANIMALS ANIMALS / EARTH SCENES

The Indonesian rat snake is a long snake with a very slender body. It lives on the ground, mainly in low-lying areas, where it is active during daylight hours. Its gray or brown body blends in with the surroundings, making it difficult to spot. Its large eyes are very useful in spotting its favorite prey—rats, mice, and other small vertebrates. The snake also has an excellent sense of smell, which it uses to trail prey.

The Indonesian rat snake is neither poisonous nor harmful to humans. It has extremely flexible jaws, which can open very, very wide. The snake grabs its prey in these strong jaws and swallows the helpless animal alive. Slender, backward-pointing teeth on the jaws prevent the prey from slipping forward out of the mouth. The only path the prey can take is inward, down the snake's throat. The throat is elastic enough to accommodate fat prey.

Male Indonesian rat snakes are generally slightly larger than the females. The males find females by the sense of smell. A female's skin gives off a scent as she crawls along. A male picks up the trail of this scent and follows it. After mating, the female lays a clutch of eggs with tough, leathery shells. Each young snake, or hatchling, cuts its way through the shell using a special "egg tooth" at the front of its upper jaw.

37

Ladder Snake
Elaphe scalaris

Length: 3 to 4 feet
Diet: mice, small birds, and lizards
Number of Eggs: 6 to 12

Home: Spain, Portugal, and southern France
Order: Lizards and snakes
Family: Colubrid snakes

 Cities, Towns, and Farms

 Reptiles

© JOSE LUIS G. GRANDE / PHOTO RESEARCHERS

The ladder snake gets its name from the distinctive pattern of colors on its body. Two bold lines run down its back. Between them are many crossbars that resemble the steps of a ladder. This ladder pattern is most clearly seen on young snakes. The steplike crossbars fade after the first few years of life, leaving only two bold racing stripes.

Young ladder snakes hatch from 2-inch-long eggs, which the female tucks under or between some rocks and stones. At first the baby snakes feed on large insects. But soon they learn to capture small lizards. As adults, ladder snakes hunt for mice and birds in daylight. At night, they retreat to warm rock crevices or mouse burrows.

The ladder snake is a real sun worshiper. Even on hot summer days, when other reptiles retreat into the shade, the ladder snake lies coiled on a sunny rock or patch of ground. It is often seen in French vineyards, basking on a warm stone wall. In Spain and Portugal, it is occasionally found in dry woodlands and along bushy hillsides.

Although it appears to be an easy prey as it lazily basks in the sun, the ladder snake is very difficult to catch. It is alert to danger and quick to flee. When cornered the snake bites. Most ladder snakes kept in terraria, or indoor tanks, remain shy throughout their lives. They may occasionally nip at their handler, however. Ladder snakes can survive in captivity if kept very dry and warm.

Lizard Snake
Malpolon monspessulanus

Method of Reproduction: egg layer
Home: southern Europe, northern Africa, the Mediterranean, and southwestern Asia

Length: 3 to 6½ feet
Diet: reptiles and small mammals
Order: Lizards and snakes
Family: Colubrid snakes

 Cities, Towns, and Farms

 Reptiles

© JUAN MANUEL BORRERO / NATURE PICTURE LIBRARY

The lizard snake races across the ground with its head held high. It scouts for prey, looking every which way with keen-sighted eyes. Though it is fastest when traveling across sand or rocks, this nimble hunter can also slither up trees or bushes. With its great speed and fine eyesight, the lizard snake can easily chase down smaller snakes, as well as lizards, mice, and other small animals. It quickly paralyzes its prey with a venomous bite. Fortunately, this large and common European snake is not so poisonous as to pose a great danger to humans. Still, one would be wise to handle it carefully.

Up close, the lizard snake can be recognized by the peculiar shape of its head. Its skull is long, and the top of its head is depressed, forming a distinctive dip between the snake's large, dramatic eyes. Two small ridges form hoods, or visors, above each eye. The lizard snake prefers to hunt under the bright midday sun. And its hooded brows help shade its eyes from glare.

The lizard snake is especially common in the dried-out fields around old and abandoned European farms. It also thrives in sandy and rocky scrublands and open woods, and around sand dunes along the Mediterranean Sea and Atlantic coast. The nonvenomous common king snake is its close cousin in North America.

Mangrove Snake
Boiga dendrophila

Length: 6 to 7 feet
Length at Hatching: 1 foot
Diet: rodents, birds, lizards, and eggs
Number of Eggs: 4 to 15

Home: Malay Peninsula, Indonesia, and the Philippines
Order: Snakes and lizards
Family: Colubrid snakes

 Forests and Mountains

 Reptiles

© BRUCE WATKINS / ANIMALS ANIMALS / EARTH SCENES

The mangrove snake is named for the mangrove tree that grows in swamps and along rivers in tropical parts of the world. During the day, mangrove snakes can often be found coiled up in these trees. The snakes are easy to catch because they do not flee when people approach—although they will bite when angered. This colorful, docile snake is a favorite of snake charmers. It can be seen performing in street shows and circus acts throughout Indonesia. At night, however, the laid-back mangrove snake becomes an aggressive hunter. It slithers though the jungle searching for small animals and kills its prey with a vicious bite. The mangrove snake's bite is venomous. Fangs in the back of its mouth inject a weak poison. Though not strong enough to kill a person, the bite of a mangrove snake can cause illness.

Like all snakes, this species periodically sheds its skin as it grows. Female mangrove snakes generally shed 8 to 11 days before laying their eggs. The mangrove snake will try to find a warm, safe place for her eggs, but she will not guard them. If they are not eaten by jungle animals, her eggs will hatch in three months.

When the hatchlings emerge, they are already several times larger than their eggs. They accomplish this by coiling up very tightly inside the shell. Mangrove snakes are born hunters. As soon as they hatch, the baby snakes can catch and eat mice and small birds.

Smooth Snake
Coronella austriaca

Length: 22 to 30 inches
Diet: lizards, blind snakes, mice, and voles
Number of Young: 2 to 18

Home: Europe and western Asia
Order: Lizards and snakes
Family: Colubrid snakes

 Forests and Mountains

 Reptiles

© GEORGE MCCARTHY / CORBIS

The smooth snake is a wimp in cobra's clothing. Although in coloration it looks much like a cobra, the smooth snake reacts to danger in a most uncobralike manner: it flees. When cornered, however, the smooth snake mimics cobra behavior. First it coils itself up. Then, in a split second, it bends back its head, hisses loudly, and strikes. A person confronted by such a display might be inclined to kill the creature. Fortunately, though, the smooth snake is utterly harmless to humans. It has no poison, and its tiny teeth can barely cause a minor wound.

The smooth snake is named for its smooth and shiny scales. The snake prefers to live in woodlands, particularly near clearings that afford areas for it to sunbathe, although it is not unusual to find the smooth snake near farms, vineyards, and rock quarries. The smooth snake hunts during the day, capturing prey by the neck and suffocating the victim between two or three coils. The snake then swallows the victim whole.

Smooth snakes hibernate during the winter. They mate in spring, soon after they emerge from hibernation. The fertilized eggs develop within the female's body. Each baby is enclosed in an eggshell, which breaks at birth. A newborn smooth snake is 6 to 8 inches long. Young smooth snakes feed on small lizards and blind snakes. As they grow bigger, they are able to catch more substantial prey.

Viperine Snake
Natrix maura

Length: 2 to 3 feet
Diet: fish, amphibians, and worms
Number of Eggs: 4 to 20

Home: southern Europe, Turkey, and northern Africa
Order: Lizards and snakes
Family: Colubrid snakes

 Fresh Water

 Reptiles

© J. C. CARTON / BRUCE COLEMAN INC.

The viperine snake never strays far from water. It is often seen rushing through a pond—its mouth wide open—in pursuit of a tasty fish. When coming up for air, this slender snake raises only its nostrils and eyes above the surface. The viperine snake likes to stand straight up in the water by resting the end of its tail on the bottom.

A voracious predator, the viperine snake can swallow a small fish in one gulp or drag a large fish ashore for a feast. Viperine snakes also prowl the muddy shoreline, searching for toads, frogs, and newts. Despite their fierceness as hunters, viperine snakes don't bite people. They make good pets that quickly learn to associate their owner with food. Viperine snakes can survive on a diet of earthworms. Unlike many snakes, they don't mind eating dead food.

The viperine snake gets its name from a pattern of black or brown marks that runs down its back. This pattern may resemble the zigzag stripe seen on true vipers. The scales on the viperine snake are slightly raised, or "keeled," which gives it the rough feel of a metal file.

After mating, viperine snakes lay their eggs in June or July. When they hatch in August, the young snakes are about 7 inches long. The males grow to between 2 and 2½ feet, but the females can get considerably larger. Old, large females can become quite long and fat.

Field Sparrow
Spizella pusilla

Length: 5¼ to 6 inches
Wingspan: 7¾ to 8½ inches
Weight: ⅓ to ½ ounce
Diet: insects, spiders, and seeds

Number of Eggs: 3 to 6
Home: eastern and central North America
Order: Perching birds
Family: Finches

Grasslands

Birds

☐ Summer
▨ Winter

© GREGORY K. SCOTT / PHOTO RESEARCHERS

Bird-watchers who gather in fields and brush woodlands to see the tiny field sparrow often have a difficult time spotting this bird. It spends much of its time on the ground hunting for beetles, grasshoppers, ants, spiders, and other food. The sparrow's rust-colored feathers blend with its surroundings and hide the bird from hawks and other predators.

Although different types of sparrows also resemble each other, you can easily identify the field sparrow by its distinctive pink beak. The males and females look alike. Field sparrows are most visible during the spring breeding season. At that time the male becomes very territorial, patrolling his nesting area like a nervous homeowner. He flies from bush to tree to fence post, all the while repeating a call that warns other field sparrows to keep their distance!

The female field sparrow builds the nest, using grass and leaves for the exterior, and soft hairs for the interior. The nest is often built on or near the ground, either, in a clump of grass or in a bush. After laying her eggs, the female incubates them for two weeks. The chicks leave the nest only seven or eight days after hatching and learn to fly when they are about two weeks old. A female field sparrow raises two or three broods of babies each year. Those field sparrows living in the northern United States migrate, flying south in the fall to warmer climates.

43

Barrel Spider (Wind Scorpion)
Galeodes sp.

Length: about 1 inch
Diet: mainly spiders, insects, and earthworms
Method of Reproduction: egg layer

Home: Asia and northern Africa
Order: Wind scorpions
Family: Galeodid wind scorpions

 Deserts

 Arthropods

© DANIEL HEUCLIN / NHPA

The wind scorpion, or barrel spider, has legs that resemble those of a spider. Its body looks more like a scorpion's. Yet it is neither spider nor scorpion. It is a unique, fast-running arachnid that lives in deserts and dry, bushy areas. The wind scorpion appears to have 10 legs. Actually, the front set of "legs" are special organs called "pedipalps." The wind scorpion's long, slender pedipalps end in sticky tips and long, sensitive hairs. The creature uses them as feelers and as hands to grip its food.

Wind scorpions are most active at night, when they scurry across the dry ground with great speed. They are always on the prowl for food and eat any animal small enough to kill. The wind scorpion has an amazing mouth. Its jaws open from side to side, rather than up and down, so it slices through its prey like a pair of sharp scissors. A large wind scorpion is capable of snipping off the tip of a human finger! When excited, the creature makes twittering sounds using special organs on its head.

Wind scorpions of the genus *Galeodes* live in the desert and grassland areas of Asia and northern Africa. Related species can be found in the arid regions of western North America, from southern Canada to Mexico. These North American wind scorpions are somewhat smaller than their Old World cousins and have stubbier legs.